FACT FINDERS

Educational adviser: Arthur Razzell

Early Aircraft

John E. Allen

Illustrated by Dick Eastland
and Eric Jewell Associates
Designed by Faulkner/Marks Partnership

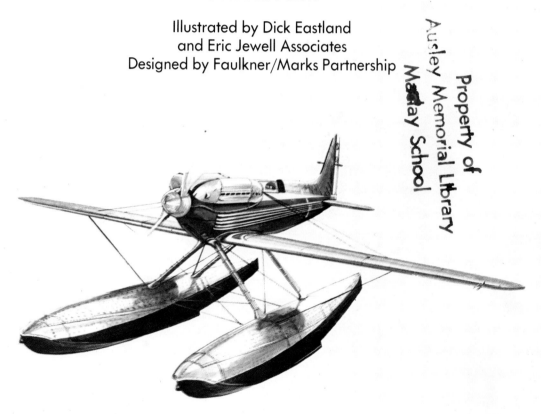

Silver Burdett Company

© 1976 Macmillan Education Limited

Published in the United
States by Silver Burdett
Company, Morristown, N.J.
1978 Printing

ISBN 0-382-06244-2

Library of Congress
Catalog Card No. 78-64653

Early Aircraft

The Pioneers

Man has always dreamed of being able to fly through the air, but it was a long time before he succeeded. Leonardo da Vinci drew sketches of flying machines, but never actually made them.

Much later, scientists made models that showed flying was possible.

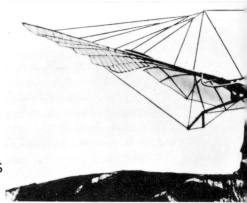

Cayley's gliders

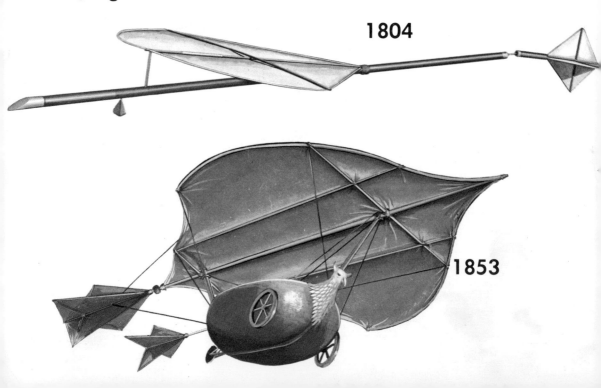

1804

1853

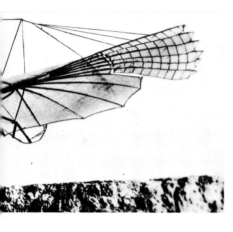

In 1804 George Cayley made a model glider. Fifty years later he made the first glider capable of carrying a person.

Otto Lilienthal (left and below) built a number of experimental gliders. He made over 2000 flights in them.

Otto Lilienthal flying one of his gliders

The First Flight

Lawrence Hargrave, an Australian, flew specially shaped box kites. These were steady and could lift heavy weights.

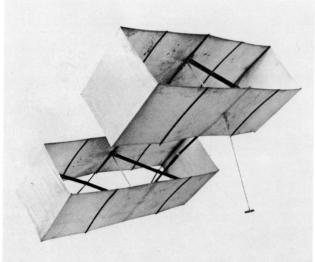

Hargrave's box kite

Orville Wright

In 1893, Hargrave took his kites to the U.S.A. They were seen by the brothers Orville and Wilbur Wright (right). The Wright brothers made a glider the same shape as the box kite.

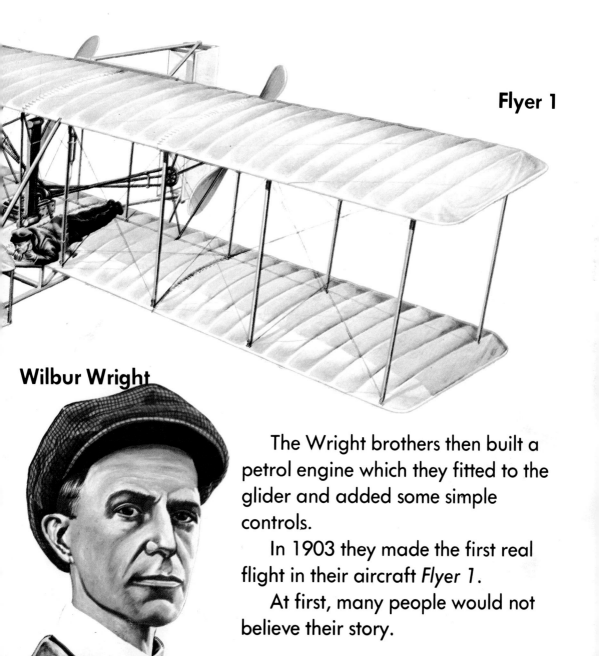

Flyer 1

Wilbur Wright

The Wright brothers then built a petrol engine which they fitted to the glider and added some simple controls.

In 1903 they made the first real flight in their aircraft *Flyer 1*.

At first, many people would not believe their story.

The Growth of Aviation

Avis Monoplane (1910)

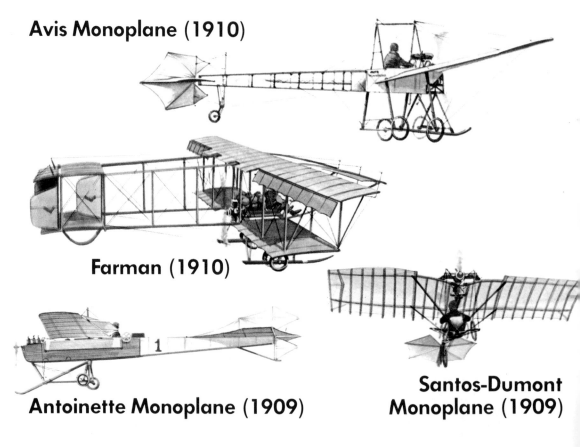

Farman (1910)

Antoinette Monoplane (1909)

Santos-Dumont Monoplane (1909)

In Europe, many people copied the Wright brothers' aircraft.

Engineers built aircraft in a great variety of shapes and sizes (above).

Soon, flying (or aviation) became a great sport and the first races took place.

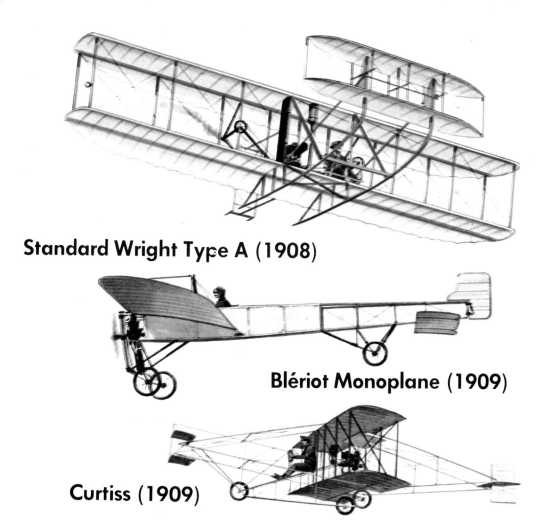

Standard Wright Type A (1908)

Blériot Monoplane (1909)

Curtiss (1909)

Pilots from many countries competed in the races. They tried to fly faster, higher, and further than the other competitors. The first aircraft companies were formed. On the left is one of the first passenger aircraft, the Russian *Ilia Mourometz*.

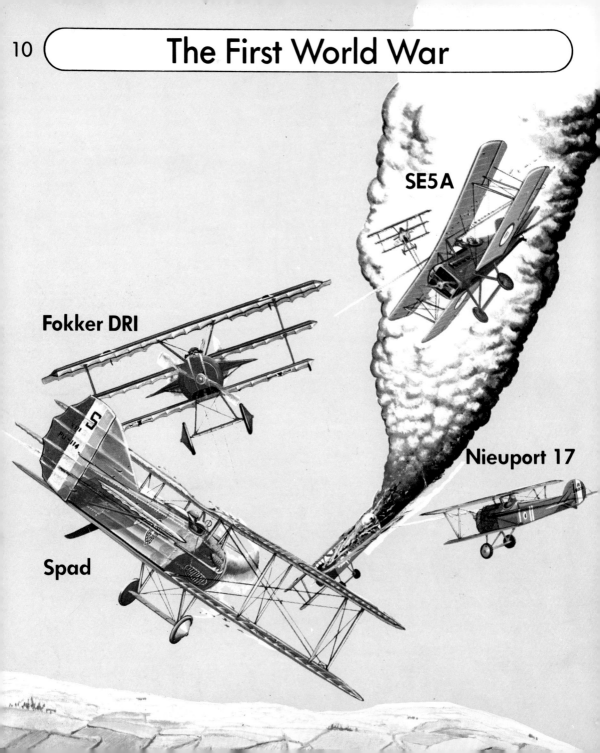

The First World War

SE5A

Fokker DRI

Nieuport 17

Spad

During the First World War (1914-1918) armies used aircraft fitted with machine guns. There were fierce air battles called 'dog fights' (opposite).

Aircraft were also used to spy on the enemy's positions.

The aircraft above is a Handley Page 0/400 bomber. Crews had to wear protective flying kit (left).

The Record Breakers

After the war, adventurous men designed and built special aircraft.

In 1927 Charles A. Lindbergh became the first person to fly across the Atlantic Ocean without stopping. He flew 6000 kilometres in $33\frac{1}{2}$ hours, in his aircraft *Spirit of St. Louis.*

The *Spirit of St. Louis* had huge petrol tanks. The pilot needed a periscope to see over them.

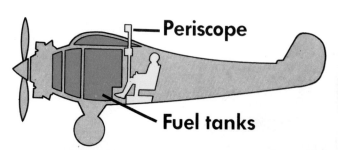

Periscope

Fuel tanks

Charles Lindbergh

There were many high speed competitions. The Schneider Trophy contests took place between 1914 and 1931. These were races especially held for seaplanes.

In 1931 the Supermarine S6B seaplane (below) reached a speed of 657 kilometres an hour.

Supermarine Seaplane (U.K.)

The First Airways

DC2 (U.S.A.)

The first airlines with fare-paying passengers started in 1919.

The first really modern airliners were the Douglas DC2 (above) and DC3. These aircraft made flying both fast and comfortable. The picture on the right shows the interior of a DC2.

Some DC2s are still flying today.

Air stewardesses (right) looked after the passengers.

Large flying boats flew from England to Australia and South Africa. They did not need an airport. They could land on the sea, or on rivers and lakes.

Empire Flying Boat (U.K.)

A kite is lifted in the air by the wind flowing past it. The wind flows past the wing of an aircraft in the same way. The wind also flows past the aircraft's tail. This points the aircraft in the right direction.

**Tail of aircraft goe
up when elevato
go dow**

**Joystick controls
ailerons and elevators**

Aileron

Coc

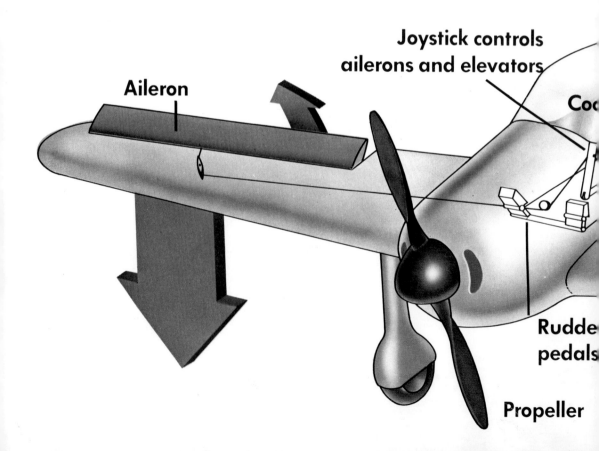

**Rudde
pedals**

Propeller

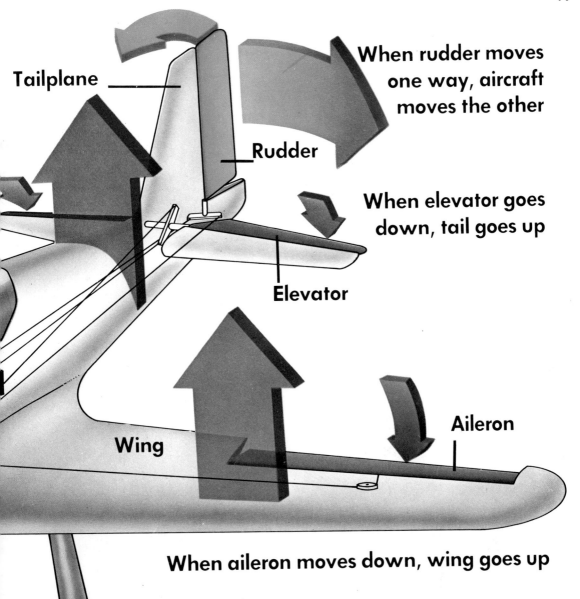

Tailplane

When rudder moves
one way, aircraft
moves the other

Rudder

When elevator goes
down, tail goes up

Elevator

Aileron

Wing

When aileron moves down, wing goes up

Landing wheel

Moving through the Air

A windmill is turned by the wind. If a windmill is driven by a motor it becomes a fan. The fan makes its own wind. Aircraft are driven through the air by propellers. These act like fans but blow the air backwards.

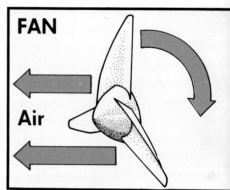

FAN

Air

A SIMPLE TOY AIRCRAFT

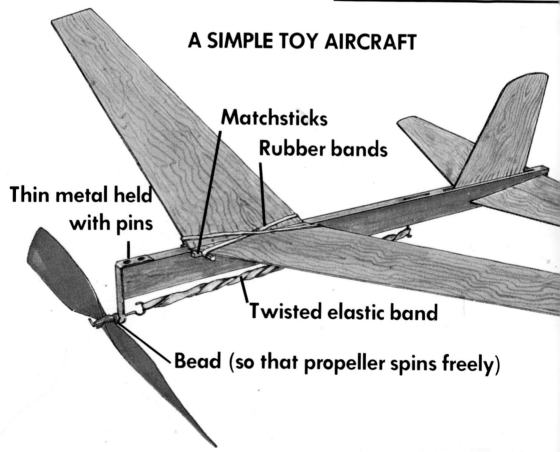

Matchsticks

Rubber bands

Thin metal held with pins

Twisted elastic band

Bead (so that propeller spins freely)

19

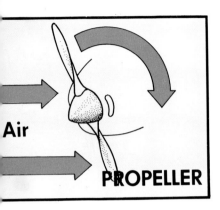

Air

PROPELLER

In a toy aircraft, the propeller may be driven by an elastic band.

In a real aircraft, the propeller is driven by a powerful engine. The picture below shows the propeller and engine of a modern light aircraft.

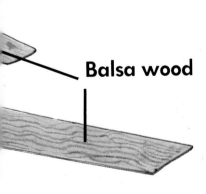

Balsa wood

The Second World War

In the Second World War, several countries built thousands of aircraft. Air battles were fought by fast fighters such as the Spitfire (below).

Large bombers flew hundreds of kilometres to drop bombs on enemy cities.

V1 (Germany) pilotless flying bomb

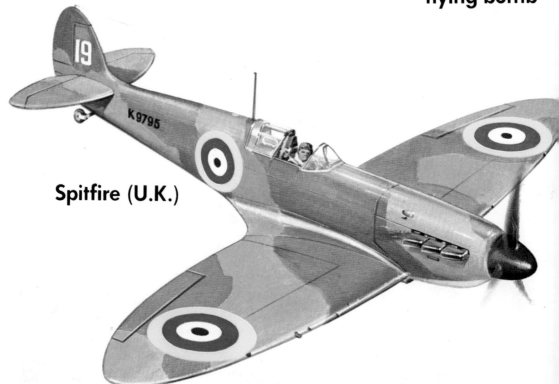

Spitfire (U.K.)

Near the end of the war, the Germans developed small rocket aircraft, like the Messerschmitt Komet (below).

Jet engines, which do not use propellers, led to much faster fighters. The V1 (left) has a jet engine.

Messerschmitt Komet (Germany)

Glossary

Ailerons   Hinged flaps on the wings of an aircraft. When the ailerons are moved, the wings go up or down.

Aircraft   A flying machine supported by the air.

Dog Fights   Air battles between fighter aircraft.

Elevators   Hinged flaps at the tail of an aircraft. When the elevators are moved the aircraft goes up or down.

Flying Kit   Special clothing worn by pilots and aircrew.

Glider   An aircraft which has no engine. A glider has fixed wings and is supported by air currents.

Jet Engine   An engine which drives an aircraft forward by pumping a jet of air backwards.

Kite   A light frame with a thin covering. A kite is flown in the air by attaching it to a tow line.

Machine Gun   An automatic gun that fires a stream of bullets.

Periscope   A tube with mirrors arranged inside. By looking through a periscope one can see over obstacles.

Propeller   An engine-driven 'screw' which pulls air towards it and so drives the aircraft forward.

Rocket Aircraft   Aircraft driven by rockets, rather than propellers or jet engines.

Seaplane   An aircraft that can land on the sea.

Index

2 3 4 5 6 7 8 9 10— R —85 84 83 82